Going Down, Friend

poems by

David James

Finishing Line Press
Georgetown, Kentucky

Going Down, Friend

ACKNOWLEDGMENTS

Bamboo Ridge: Going Down, Friend
Barking Sycamores: Immortality and Truth
Connecticut River Review: The Poem You Did Not Ask For
Connotation: A Little Known Fact
Heron Tree: Camus Re-invented in Linden, Michigan
Old Northwest Review: Is it Me
Poem: It Goes On
Poetry East: There Comes a Time When You Have to Put Your Love into Words
South Carolina Review: My Heart Breaks

Publisher: Leah Maines

Editor: Christen Kincaid

Cover Art: Pixabay and CC0

Author Photo: David James

Cover Design: Elizabeth Maines McCleavy

Printed in the USA on acid-free paper.
Order online: www.finishinglinepress.com
also available on amazon.com

Author inquiries and mail orders:
Finishing Line Press
P. O. Box 1626
Georgetown, Kentucky 40324
U. S. A.

Table of Contents

Camus Re-invented in Linden, Michigan 1

The Poem You Did Not Ask For 2

Dead at X and Y 3

How I Met Your Mother 4

Each Branch Turns 5

Don't Listen 6

My Heart Breaks 7

A Little Known Fact 8

Is it Me 9

It Goes On 10

Love, That 11

How the World Does Not Work 12

Interview with My Dying Self 13

There Comes a Time When You Have to Put

    Your Love into Words 14

The Older I Get, the More I Feel 15

Immortality and Truth.. 17

Going Down, Friend 18

Dedicated to my Mom and Dad for showing me
what is important in life
With thanks also to one of my brothers, Tom Heideman,
for inspiring the title poem

CAMUS RE-INVENTED IN LINDEN, MICHIGAN

"If I were a tree among trees, a cat among animals, this life
would have meaning…for I should belong to this world."
Albert Camus, from "The Myth of Sisyphus"

The apple tree blossoms fall like snowflakes,

a soft, white carpet on the patio cement.
Wind or no wind, they drift down

like tiny birds, eyeing bread crumbs below,
praising the sun and blue sky
pulled over a spring day in this quiet town.

I sit under the tree and petals land on me,
on my paper, on my shoulders and head.
In two or three days,
I'd be covered completely.

Maybe then I'd belong here, not misled

by fear, not worrying about the money
to retire or whether I can fix the pool light.

I wouldn't care about the need for oil changes or new brakes,
the mild ache in my back, my right knee
grinding bone on bone. The sun would set, night

would crawl in on its dark belly.
I would know what to do, the way
the apple tree sits alone and lets the wind and birds
do their jobs in a warm heaven full of bees.

THE POEM YOU DID NOT ASK FOR
inspired by "The Poem You Asked For" by Larry Levis

This one is a stalker.
In the shadows, at the back table of the coffee shop,

standing off in the distance, staring your way,
the poem follows your trends, your comings and goings,

when you walk out to the mailbox, where you stop
for gas. It passes you on the highway,

brings you that extra fork when you drop yours
at the restaurant. It watches through the back window

as you sing, washing dishes at the sink.
The minute you let your guard down and ignore

the obvious, the poem unloads
its bags, moves in like a ghost, undercover.

Now it can walk into your dreams, slide under your skin.
It can hide in the back of your brain like your first love,

a love from which you never quite recovered.

DEAD AT X AND Y

"If the heart stops beating," explains a state wildlife veterinarian,
"it sends a text message to our phone that says, 'I'm dead at x and y
coordinates.'" from "Findings," Harper's, Dec. 2013

Used in Minnesota first to monitor
moose mortality rates, the idea has spread
to humans, mostly the elderly.
Family members can now receive a phone text
telling them that grandpa is dead
and where to find his body.

Death doesn't have to be a surprise anymore.
You're spared that difficult phone call from someone
crying and weeping, barely audible.

You'll know the minute he collapses on the floor.

HOW I MET YOUR MOTHER

Everything's late this year
after such a cold winter, brutal temperatures
and record snowfall. Sure, the tulips are up, like always,
with a few daffodils, but the apple tree
doesn't have one white flower yet.
The rose bushes look dead. Of course,
that could be true. Like a sorry gambler,
you've planted four tomato plants in large vases,
though none of your plants produced last year,
or the year before.

You'd think you'd learn, but spring comes
and makes fools of everyone.
There's a gene for hope that lights up
when birds wake you in the morning,
the grass is green again and needs cutting,
when it's a sunny day, mid-70's,
and the ribs on the grill send smoke
in your eyes.

Spring's a time when anything seems possible,
even love, and you go on a diet, start the push-ups,
begin to consider what you'll wear to work—
maybe that blue shirt and tie to impress
the new hire in the office, the one
whose red hair is on fire,
who with one quick glance
burns that last bit of ice
off your heart.

EACH BRANCH TURNS

"On your piano a plaster Beethoven stands
and thinks: Thank goodness I've gone deaf."
from "Picture Postcard from Our Youth," Dan Pagis

Our picture of Mother Teresa weeps
every evening as we sit
comfortably in our home, reading, surfing the net,

debating whether we'll need a sleep-
ing pill tonight, or not. Our neighbor lady died
this morning, found by her son under a yellow knit

blanket. At 94, it's a blessing, but it still burns.
On the wall, the statue of Jesus on a cross
lifts his head and watches the woman's spirit

rise while the EMTs slide
her tiny body on a stretcher. We all learn
the language of loss in time.

Jesus has stopped wondering how long he'll have to hang here.
Birds sing. The apple tree blooms. Each branch turns
away from the dead of winter, reaches up, opens wide.

DON'T LISTEN

Don't listen to me. And don't read my poems.
They're full of lies, dreams, wishes. They'll take
you down the primrose path, only to get you drunk
and lost, calling out for your mommy.
          Think of me as a rattlesnake,
making music but poisonous. My images flunk
every test of decency. My rhymes are way off.
Who am I to capture truth and reason?
I stumble forward like everyone else down here,
half-blind, starving, drinking mud from the trough
of ignorance.   Life is one long trial for treason,
and the verdict is six-feet under.
                              No one escapes.
          Walk your own road. Write your own poetry.
It's December for me, a light snow, and in the distance, thunder.

MY HEART BREAKS

"you know it's the darkness of your own heart healing…"
from "The Tree, the Lamp," Yves Bonnefoy

The heart was born to break,
shatter into a million pieces, and then assemble itself

into a heart again, only to fall
and break. There's no other way down here.

The heart walks to the edge, calls for help,
and then leaps into the darkness. It's all

or nothing.
Some wags try to keep their hearts safe, chained,

tied to a tree, buried in work or hobbies.
But the snow always melts, the sun rises, spring

arrives and the heart wanders free in the rain.
It finds a bridge, a cliff, a roof, and jumps again,

happy for a moment in the slow fall.
It breaks. It heals.

Today, love, in your arms, my heart in on the mend.

A LITTLE KNOWN FACT

*"A dead hummingbird was reported to have been found in
the pocket of a dead man in the Sonoran Desert."
from Harper's, "Findings," March 2013*

It's an obscure, ancient suicide technique—
capture a hummingbird and place it in your pocket.

In its attempt to escape,
the tiny bird flutters and buzzes back and forth,

and you're lulled
into a trance. You forget

whatever life you had, your brain slate
wiped clean. You lie down, close your eyes,

and as the bird dies from exhaustion,
you smile. The sky opens its huge mouth.

Every terrible knot in your body is slowly untied.

IS IT ME

or has the day shrunk to 22 hours
and fifty minutes? Are birds a little harder to hear?
Do trees look at you with a quiet sadness?
Is the moon inching closer? Do you think all flowers
smell like frozen raspberries?   Some days,
I swear the world is against me, trying to smear
what's left of my good name in mud.

Maybe this is how it should be—at a certain age, we push
people down the hill, distance ourselves, turn and steer
our busy lives away
so we don't have to watch them get cut
down; we don't have to admit we're on the same path.

Do falling leaves call your name as they hit the ground?
Does the morning rain feel warm and taste like blood?
Is it just me or are my feet sinking in wet clay?

IT GOES ON

The maple leaves
stain half-yellow overnight
and drop like flies,
flies drawn by pre-schoolers
cut out on green and yellow paper.
The paper floats on a calm ocean
of grass that needs cutting.
Finally got my hair cut yesterday
and found out the barber's
parents are 97 and 95,
married for 72 years so far.
My father, on oxygen now, 81,
believes with all of his heart
that he's going deer hunting,
though he can't walk out
to the mailbox and back.
He can't hold up a rifle
long enough to aim and shoot.
I shot my first deer at 14, a button buck.
My grandpa passed me the bottle
of Southern Comfort.
There is a certain peace
sitting out in the back yard like this,
watching the steady rain of leaves,
wondering how they know when to let go,
how it feels
to fly for a while,
and then let the earth do its one and only job.

LOVE, THAT

She stares outside at the hard snowfall
blowing sideways, twenty degrees.

She knows nothing about the science of global warming,
only that it was 55 yesterday with thunder
and lightning. Today, there's enough snow to ski

into town. Who knows what will happen by evening?
For some unknown reason, the woman makes

a connection between the weather and her life.
It's warm, it's cold. Men come and go and she never knows why.
One week, she's falling in love, laughing, fixing baked

Alaska, and in two days, she sits with a knife
at her wrist, wondering what's the fucking point

of having her heart stepped on, kicked down the road.
For a whole month, she swears off love,
tired of how it burns and disappoints.

One afternoon, a man smiles at her and her heart explodes,
the weather changes on a dime.

Rain. Snow. Lightning. Ice. Floods. Ten below.
Love starts, stops. Love pours down in buckets. Love dries up.
That beautiful savior, love. Love, that lonely crime.

HOW THE WORLD DOES NOT WORK

"trying to hang the fruit back on the trees"
John Glenday

Isn't this what we all do, sooner or later,
try to take back the mistakes, the words said
in anger, the sins that haunt our dreams?
But the world won't slow down, and certainly
won't back itself up. It barrels on, fed
by our breath, by our hearts' steady routine.

When I hold you in my arms and stand,
smelling your hair, feeling your body
cave against mine, I like to believe
that, somewhere, a rock crumbles back to sand,
that a maple tree collapses into a seed.

In my dreams, I return the apples to the high
branches, the petals to their flower stems. I squeeze
the robin back into its egg and imagine a bird's song
dissolving in the wide open sky.

INTERVIEW WITH MY DYING SELF

This should come as no surprise—
I've known since day one the end
would stop me in mid-step;

I just never believed it would happen. There's no prep
for those few awkward moments before you spend
your last breath, your body collapsing, your eyes

glazing over, still open. If only I had listened
to those before me. I wasted so much time
on revenge and anger, on worrying about money

or bills, what other people thought. It's funny
but now that I'm dying, I see how softly the light shines
in the window, how every desire sails away in the wind.

THERE COMES A TIME WHEN YOU HAVE
TO PUT YOUR LOVE INTO WORDS

I'll suck the blue out of the sky
& let you drink it down with sunlight
& bird calls. I'll make little square mints from clouds,

dreams, maple trees & the smiles of strangers,
& you can eat them until you're full & happy.
I'll erase every ache & pain, carve what is wrong into right

by pulling stars out of the night sky, one by one,
rubbing their faces in my hands
until only good wishes remain. I know it sounds sappy,

but love carries all things in its mouth & sprays it
on those who look up & believe.
The future is buried in what we love. Take my hand

& the earth will spin us like golden tops.
Hold me & death himself will look the other way,
curse his fate. Kiss me, love, & the breeze

will lift us out of this skin, out of these bulky bodies.
The world will turn but around us, standing there
at the center of all things worthy of praise.

THE OLDER I GET, THE MORE I FEEL

a quickness in my step, in my
staring at November's leafy mess, in the
urge to get something *done*. In the apples

I need to pick up, compost. In the roses
to trim and cover. In the garden that needs
fertilizer, turning, some infusion of rich

minerals that will soak into the dirt
and help my vegetables next spring.
In the one row of parsley still trying

to grow through the freezing temperatures at night.
On the side wall of my heart,
where my grandson spray paints an elk and T-rex

walking side-by-side, I'm slowly losing
everything I want to remember.
It's no use, says a blue jay.

Let it go, says the harvest moon, stuck
on a house two streets over.
The wind blows in from only God knows where

and shakes my confidence down from the low branches,
sings of all we can't know, but wonder,
all we can't see, but feel,

all we can't ask, but understand.
The maples shine in the moonlight,
empty and shivering.

Another day scrapes its fingers
across my face and disappears into shadows.
My star in the night sky

shrinks a bit with every sunset,
every sunrise. I'm falling
and that's no longer a metaphor. The earth

rises to swallow me. I smell the cut grass
and crumbling leaves in the rain.
In Minnesota, the first snow cloud forms

and heads this way. The truth is simple:
I'm not ready for snow yet, but I sure as hell
want to be here when it

                          falls.

IMMORTALITY AND TRUTH
"Children's belief in immortality is universal."
from "Findings," Harper's, April 2014

Hell, we all think
we'll live forever, even that old guy in hospice,
confessing to the nurses that it's all an elaborate hoax,
that one day soon, he'll stand up and dance his way
out the front doors, flashing his middle finger
at death. Dying is an accident, something done
by people who aren't careful,
people who are stupid and drive their cars into trees,
people who are in the wrong places
at the wrong times.
Most of my life so far, I've been in the right place
at the right time, and that's how I plan to keep it.
No hospitals, no hospices. Ten and two on the steering wheel,
a decent distance between me and the car in front.
No heroin or cocaine, no crystal meth. A baby's aspirin
every day, vitamin C every other.
No combat or war zones, no swimming with the sharks,
no tightrope on the 18th floor after drinking, no prostitutes
on Gratiot Avenue, no karaoke with gang-bangers,
no Russian roulette, dynamite, nuclear fission,
no Rottweilers, no knife-throwing friends.
I'm just a big old kid and immortality's my middle name.
If I do die, by mistake, my belief in God and the afterlife
will hold me up, propel me into forever land where I can lounge
on a cloud, throw lightning bolts, fly through the heavens,
float down to earth and make wishes come true for those
who can't see me but still believe.
And if that doesn't happen, if all this *is* an elaborate hoax,
then when I die, if I die,
I'm going to be one pissed-off dude.

GOING DOWN, FRIEND
for Tom H.

We're all going down, friend, so go down swinging.
Fuck the ringing in your ears. Fuck the past
drooling out of your brain.

Fuck every little regret crawling into the corner
of your memory. Lift the mast
and sail your boat into open waters. Fuck the rain

and wind. Fuck the compass that doesn't work.
We're stuck down here without a clue or map,
so grab what you need, what you want, and enjoy the ride,

face held high in the mist, pretending nothing can hurt
you.   Fuck the icebergs. Fuck the straps
tied to your arms and legs. They vanish

the minute you ignore them. Turn starboard
and follow the crosswinds. The world sets a table
for you, bread and wine, green beans, grilled whitefish.

Sit down and eat. Or take the guitar, play some chords,
and write another song or three. Hell, write a symphony.
Fuck the critics. Fuck the crowd. Pick up your dream and run

with it through the thickets, the swamps, the locked doors,
the nights filled with doubt. In fact, fuck doubt. Let it bleed.

David James' books include *A Heart Out of This World, She Dances Like Mussolini,* and *My Torn Dance Card.* He's also published five chapbooks: *Do Not Give Dogs What is Holy, I Dance Back, I Will Peel This Mask Off, Trembling in Someone's Palm* and *No Way to Stop the Bleeding.*

In addition to publishing poetry, more than thirty of James' one-act plays have been produced from New York City to California. He has degrees from Western Michigan University, Central Michigan University and Wayne State University and teaches at Oakland Community College in Michigan.

James is married, has three grown children, and revels in the lives of his five grandchildren: Cloud, Chloe, Henry, Simon and Elliot. Pictures available upon request.